Self-Scoring

IQ

||||||||||||||||||||||||||||||||||||||||||||||||| Tests

Victor Serebriakoff
HONORARY INTERNATIONAL PRESIDENT, MENSA

STERLING

New York / London
www.sterlingpublishing.com

Published by Sterling Publishing Co., Inc.
387 Park Avenue South, New York, NY 10016

© 1968, 1988, 1996 by Victor Serebriakoff
Compilation © 1996 by Sterling Publishing Co., Inc.
This 1996 edition published by Sterling Publishing Co., Inc.,
by arrangement with Constable & Robinson Ltd.

Distributed in Canada by Sterling Publishing
c/o Canadian Manda Group, 165 Dufferin Street,
Toronto, Ontario, Canada M6K 3H6

Distributed in the United Kingdom by GMC Distribution Services,
Castle Place, 166 High Street, Lewes, East Sussex, England BN7 1XU

Distributed in Australia by Capricorn Link (Australia) Pty. Ltd.
P.O. Box 704, Windsor, NSW 2756, Australia

ISBN: 978-0-7607-0164-5

52

For information about custom editions, special sales, premium and
corporate purchases, please contact Sterling Special Sales Department
at 800-805-5489 or specialsales@sterlingpub.com.

Disclaimer:
These tests are not meant to replace a professional examination. The accepted view is
that the only valid test is an individual test administered by a qualified professional.

INTRODUCTION

The philosopher Aristotle once said, "Know thyself." This advice may be the most difficult to follow of any ever given.

Psychology is man's discipline for studying his own mind. It is categorized as a "soft" science, as opposed to the "hard" sciences—such as physics and chemistry—because it has not been possible to formulate exact predictive laws. However, if any branch of psychology has enough precision to claim scientific status, it is *psychometrics*, the science of mental measurement.

The pioneering work of Galton, Binet, Terman, Spearman, and Cattell has been consolidated over the past eighty years. There are few serious students of the subject who reject the value of the mental measurement known as the Intelligence Quotient or IQ test. Despite arguments concerning validity, the scientific community makes increasing use of these tests.

This booklet aims to meet the growing interest in the subject as well as to provide the general public with the opportunity to test its own intelligence. The test is similar to the elaborate standardized tests that are available for administration by professional psychologists only. Please note that the tests in this booklet have not been subjected to the usual rigorous statistical analyses conducted on very large sample groups that are necessary for a truly reliable assessment. The tests will, however, provide the best approximation of IQ that a person can obtain without going to a professional examiner. The tests are closely modeled on well-established but confidential tests.

Although all kinds of abilities vary from individual to individual, intelligence tests show that there is a clustering tendency between cognitive skills, reasoning, quick-learning capability, and problem solving. If you're good at reasoning, you'll probably be good at other cognitive tasks.

At the very least, taking this test will give you, the participant, a sense of your intellectual capabilities.

It may even bring you that much closer to fulfilling Aristotle's command to "Know thyself."

Victor Serebriakoff
Honorary International President, MENSA
1995

Cognitive Test A

Test begins here

PRACTICE VERBAL TEST
18 questions. No time limit. Try to practice working quickly.

PV = Practice Verbal Test

Analogies I

This is an analogy: **dark is to light as black is to white**.

Complete each following analogy by underlining two words from those in parentheses.

Example: high is to low as (sky, earth, tree, plant: sky is analogous to earth)

PV 1   dog is to puppy as (pig, cat, kitten)

PV 2   circle is to globe as (triangle, square, solid, cube)

Similarities

Underline the two words in each line with the most similar meanings.

Example: mat, linoleum, floor, rug (mat is similar to rug)

PV 3   large, all, big

PV 4   empty, wide, entire, whole

Comprehension

Read the following passage. The spaces may be filled from the list underneath. In each space write the letter of the word which would best fill the space. No word should be used more than once and some are not needed at all. The first letter is inserted as an example.

PV 5, 6 and six little (. .B. .) of silvery mist (. . . .) to drift through the hollows while the light (. . . . .) after sunset.

(A) eroded, (B) wisps, (C) before, (D) ended, (E) began, (F) faded.

Odd one out

In each group of words underline the two words whose meanings do not belong with the meanings of the other words.

Example: robin, pigeon, spade, fork, eagle

PV 7   man, cod, herring, boy, flounder

PV 8   nose, mouth, smile, eyes, frown

Links

Write in the parentheses one word which means the same in one sense as the word on the left, and in another sense the same as the word on the right. The number of spaces in the parentheses corresponds to the number of letters missing.

Example: invoice (**B** i l **L**) beak

PV 9   summit (**T** _ **P**) spinning-toy

PV 10   spot (_ _**T**) Dorothy

Analogies II

Complete each analogy by writing in the parentheses one word which ends with the letter printed.

Example: high is to low as sky is to (e a r t **H**)

PV 11   young is to old as boy is to (_ _ **N**)

PV 12   airplane is to bird as submarine is to (_ _ _ **H**)

Opposites

In each line below underline the two words that are most nearly opposite in meaning.
Example: heavy, large, light

PV 13   bold, bad, timid

PV 14   tense, terse, serious, relaxed, provoked

Mid-terms

In each row, three terms on the right should correspond to three terms on the left. Insert the missing midterm on the right.

Example: first (second) third :: one (T w o) three

PV 15   mile (foot) inch :: ton (P_ _ _ _) ounce

PV 16   triangle (square) pentagon : : three (**F** _ _ _) five

Similar or opposite

In each row below underline two words that mean most nearly either the opposite or the same as each other.

Examples: 1. <u>mat</u>, linoleum, <u>rug</u>
2. <u>hate</u>, <u>love</u>, affection

PV 17   reply, punish, repute, reward

PV 18   disdain, feign, pretend, flatter

END OF PRACTICE VERBAL TEST.

Answers to practice verbal test

PV   1   cat, kitten

PV   2   square, cube (a circle is a flat shape produced from a globe, and a square is a flat shape produced from a cube)

PV   3   large, big

PV   4   entire, whole

PV   5   E (began)

PV   6   F (faded)

PV   7   man, boy (human beings, not fish)

PV   8   smile, frown (expressions, not features)

PV   9   top

PV 10   dot

PV 11   man

PV 12   fish

PV 13   bold, timid

PV 14   tense, relaxed

PV 15   pound

PV 16   four

PV 17   punish, reward (opposites)

PV 18   feign, pretend (synonyms)

You have finished the practice test. Now make sure you have a half hour free from the risk of interruption for the timed test.

VERBAL TEST A

Begin by writing down the exact time. You must complete the following 50 questions in half an hour.

VA = Verbal Test A

Analogies I

There are four terms in analogies. The first is related to the second in the same way that the third is related to the fourth. Complete each analogy by underlining two words from the four in brackets.

Example: high is to low as (<u>sky</u>, <u>earth</u>, tree, plant)

VA 1   sitter is to chair as (teacup, saucer, plate, leg)

VA 2   needle is to thread as (cotton, sew, leader, follower)

VA 3   better is to worse as (rejoice, choice, bad, mourn)

VA 4   floor is to support as (window, glass, view, brick)

VA 5   veil is to curtain as (eyes, see, window, hear)

Similarities

Underline the two words in each line with the most similar meanings.

Example: <u>mat</u>, linoleum, floor, <u>rug</u>

VA 6   divulge, divert, reveal, revert

VA 7   blessing, bless, benediction, blessed

VA 8   intelligence, speediness, currents, tidings

VA 9   tale, novel, volume, story

VA 10   incarcerate, punish, cane, chastise

Comprehension

Read this incomplete passage. The spaces in the passage are to be filled by words from the list beneath. In each space write the letter of the word that would most suitably fill the space. No word should be used more than once and some are not needed at all.

VA11-20   A successful author is (. . . .) in danger of the (. . . .) of his fame whether he continues or ceases to (. . . .). The regard of the (. . . .) is not to be maintained but by tribute, and the (. . . .) of past service to them will quickly languish (. . . .) some (. . . .) performance back to the rapidly (. . . .) minds of the masses the (. . . .) upon which the (. . . .) is based.

(A) neither, (B) fame, (C) diminution, (D) public, (E) remembrance, (F) equally, (G) new, (H) unless, (I) forgetful, (J) unreal, (K) merit, (L) write

Odd ones out

In each group of words below underline the two words whose meanings do not belong with the others.

Example: robin, pigeon, <u>space</u>, <u>fork</u>, eagle

VA 21   shark, sea lion, cod, whale, flounder

VA 22   baize, paper, felt, cloth, tinfoil

VA 23   sword, arrow, dagger, bullet, club

VA 24   bigger, quieter, nicer, quick, full

VA 25   stench, fear, sound, warmth, love

Links

Write in the brackets one word that means the same in one sense as the word on the left and in another sense the same as the word on the right.

Example: check (**B** i l **L**) beak

VA 26   dash (**D** _ _ **T**) missile

VA 27   mold (**F** _ _ **M**) body

VA 28   squash (**P** _ _ _ **S**) crowd

VA 29   thin (**F** _ _ **E**) good

VA 30   ignite (**F** _ _ **E**) shoot

Opposites

In each line below underline the two words that are most nearly opposite in meaning.

Example: <u>heavy</u>, large, <u>light</u>

VA 31   insult, deny, denigrate, firm, affirm

VA 32   missed, veil, confuse, secret, expose

VA 33   frank, humble, plain, simple, secretive

VA 34   aggravate, please, enjoy, improve, like

VA 35   antedate, primitive, primeval, primate, ultimate

Midterms

In each line, three terms on the right should correspond with three terms on the left. Insert the missing midterm on the right.

Example: first (second) third : : one (**T** w o) three

VA 36   past (present) future : : was (**I** _) will be

VA 37   complete (incomplete) blank : : always (**S** _ _ _ _ _ _ _) never

VA 38   glut (scarcity) famine :: many (**F** _ _) none

VA 39   rushing (passing) enduring : : evanescent (**T** _ _ _ _ _ _ _) eternal

VA 40   nascent (mature) senile : : green (**R** _ _ _) decayed

Similar or opposite

In each line below underline two words that mean most nearly either the opposite or the same as each other.

Examples: (a) <u>mat</u>, linoleum, <u>rug</u>, (b) <u>hate</u>, affection, <u>love</u>

VA 41   rapport, mercurial, happy, rapacious, phlegmatic

VA 42   object, deter, demur, defer, oblate

VA 43   tenacious, reprobate, irresolute, solution, tenacity

VA 44   real, renal, literally, similarly, veritably

VA 45   topography, heap, prime, plateau, hole

Analogies II

Complete each analogy by writing in the parentheses one word that ends with the letters printed.

Example: high is to low as sky is to (e a r **T H**)

VA 46   proud is to humble as generous is to (_ _ _ _ _ _ **H**)

VA 47   brave is to fearless as daring is to (_ _ _ _ _ _ **I D**)

VA 48   lend is to borrow as harmony is to (_ _ _ _ _ _ **D**)

VA 49   rare is to common as friendly is to (_ _ _ **O F**)

VA 50   skull is to brain as shell is to (_ _ _ **K**)

END OF VERBAL TEST A.
ANSWERS: page 26.

PRACTICE NUMBER TEST

Test begins here

26 questions. No time limit. Practice working quickly.

PN = Practice Number Test

Equations

In each of the following equations there is one missing number, which should be written into the parentheses.

PN 1 $21 - 6 = 3 \times (\ldots)$

PN 2 $48 \div 2 = 20 + (\ldots)$

PN 3 $4 \times 0.5 = 0.25 \times (\ldots)$

Targets

In each set of missiles there are rules that allow the target number of the missile to be formed from the numbers in the tail and wings. In the example the rule is: add the wing numbers and multiply by the tail number to get the target number. Write the answer in the blank target.

Example:

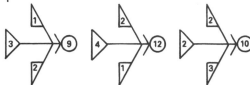

PN4

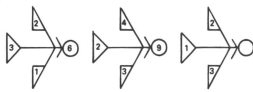

PN5

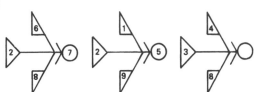

Series I

Each row of numbers below forms a series. Write in the brackets at the end of each line the number that logically should follow in the series.

Example: 1, 2, 4, (. .8. .)

PN 6   2, 4, 6, 8, (. . . .)

PN 7   18, 27, 36, (. . . .)

PN 8   81, 64, 49, 36, (. . . .)

Double rows

In each set of numbers below the same rules apply within each set to produce the numbers in the circles. Whether a number is in an upper or a lower row shows which rule applies to that number. In the example, the upper numbers in a set are added and then multiplied by the lower number to give the answer in the circle. Write the correct number in each blank circle.

Example

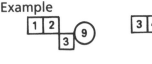

PN9

PN10

Midterms

In each line below the set of three numbers on the left is related in the same way as the set of three numbers should be on the right. Write the missing middle number on the right.

Example: 2(6)3 : : 3(12)4

PN 11   11(12)13 : : 4( )6

PN 12   4(9)5 : : 2( )3

PN 13   25(5)5 : : 24( )4

Pies

In each diagram below the numbers run in pairs or in series going around or across the diagram. Insert the missing number in the blank sector.

Example

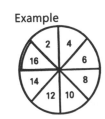

PN14

PN15

Matrices

In each square below the numbers run down and across following simple rules. In the example, the numbers in each row are formed by adding 1 to each previous number and the numbers in each column are formed by adding 2 to each previous number. Insert the missing number in the blank square.

Example:

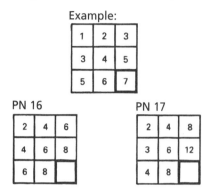

PN 16   PN 17

Squares and triangles

In each set of squares the numbers are related by particular rules to produce the number in the triangle. The items in each row follow the same rule, but the rules change from row to row. In the example, we add the numbers in the first two squares and subtract the number in the third square to give the number in the triangle. Write the missing figure into the blank triangle in each row.

Example:

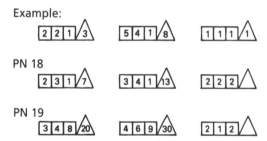

PN 18

PN 19

Rules and shapes

The shapes tell us the rules of arithmetic applying to the number. In each set, the numbers enclosed by shapes are used to produce the number not completely enclosed. Write in the missing number in each row.

Example:

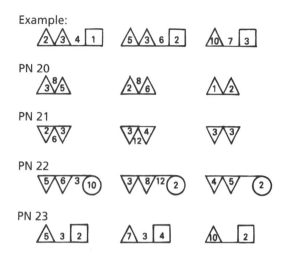

PN 20

PN 21

PN 22

PN 23

Double squares

The numbers in each row run in series. Write the two numbers that should appear in the blanks on the right-hand double square. In the example, the left-hand numbers increase by one at each step. The right-hand numbers are multiplied by two at each step.

Example:

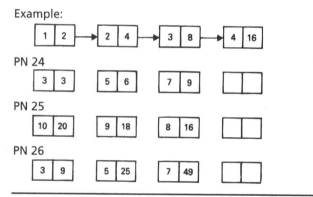

PN 24

PN 25

PN 26

END OF PRACTICE NUMBER TEST.

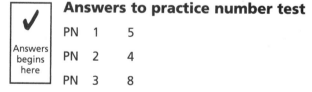

	Answers to practice number test
✓	PN 1 5
Answers begins here	PN 2 4
	PN 3 8

PN 4   6 (add numbers in wings and tail)

PN 5   4 (add numbers in wings and divide the result by the number in the tail)

PN 6   10 (add twos)

PN 7   45 (add nines)

PN 8   25 (the numbers in the series are the squares of 9, 8, 7, and 6, and the square of 5 is 25)

PN 9　5 (add numbers in upper row and subtract number in lower)

PN 10　3 (multiply numbers in upper row and divide by number in lower)

PN 11　5 (5 stands in the normal sequence of counting, between 4 and 6)

PN 12　5 (add the outer numbers to give the inner)

PN 13　6 (divide the left outer number by the right outer number)

PN 14　8 or 0 (add one to each number successively in a clockwise direction)

PN 15　2 (each pair of diagonally opposite numbers totals nine)

PN 16　10 (both rows and columns progress by adding twos)

PN 17　16 (rows progress by doubling; columns progress by doubling not the original numbers but the numbers that are to be added to make the progression)

PN 18　6 (multiply the first two numbers and add the third)

PN 19　3 (multiply the first and third numbers and subtract the second)

PN 20　3 (numbers enclosed within triangles to be added)

PN 21　9 (numbers enclosed within reversed triangles to be multiplied)

PN 22　10 (numbers enclosed within reversed triangles to be multiplied and product divided by numbers within circles)

PN 23　8 (numbers within squares to be subtracted from numbers within triangles)

PN 24　9 and 12 (the first numbers in successive double squares form a series progressing by adding twos, and the second numbers similarly by adding threes)

PN 25　7 and 14 (the first numbers progress by subtracting ones, and the second by subtracting twos)

PN 26　9 and 81 (the first numbers in successive double squares form a series by adding twos and the second numbers are the squares of corresponding first numbers)

You have finished the practice test. Now make sure you have a half hour free from the risk of interruption for the timed test.

NUMBER TEST A

Test begins here

Begin by writing down the exact time. You must complete the following 50 questions in half an hour.

NA = Number Test A

Equations
In each of the following equations there is one missing number that should be written between the brackets.

Example: $2 \times 12 = 6 \times (\overset{4}{.} . .)$

NA　1　$8 \times 7 = 14 \times (. . . .)$

NA　2　$12 + 8 - 21 = 16 + (. . . .)$

NA　3　$0.0625 \times 8 = 0.025 \div (. . . .)$

NA　4　$0.021 \div 0.25 = 0.6 \times 0.7 \times (. . . .)$

NA　5　$256 \div 64 = 512 \times (. . . .)$

Targets
In each set of missiles there are rules that allow the target number of the missile to be formed from the number in the tail and wings. In the example the rule is: add the wing numbers and multiply by the tail number to get the target number. Write the answer in the blank target.

Example:

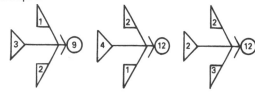

NA 6

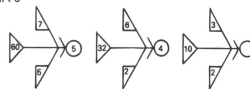

NA 7

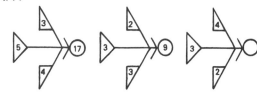

Series I

Each row of numbers forms a series. Write in the brackets the number that logically follows.

Example: 1, 2, 4, (. .8. .)

NA 8   3, 6, 12, 24, (. . . .)

NA 9   81, 54, 36, 24, (. . . .)

NA 10   2, 3, 5, 9, 17, (. . . .)

NA 11·   7, 13, 19, 25, (. . . .)

NA 12   9, 16, 25, 36, (. . . .)

Double rows

In each set of numbers below, the same rules apply within each set to produce the numbers in the circles. Whether a number is in an upper or a lower row shows which rule applies to that number. In the example the upper numbers in a set are added and then multiplied by the lower number to give the answer in the circle. Write the correct number in each blank circle.

Example

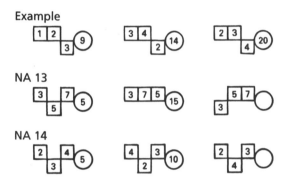

NA 13

NA 14

Midterms

In each line below the three numbers on the left are related in the same way as the three numbers should be on the right. Write the missing middle number on the right.

Example: 2 (6) 3 : : 3 (12) 4

NA 15   7 (12) 5 : : 8 (. . . .) 3

NA 16   3 (6) 2 : : 3 (. . . .) 3

NA 17   36 (14) 64 : : 16 (. . . .) 144

NA 18   294 (147) 588 : : 504 (. . . .) 168

NA 19   132 (808) 272 : : 215 (. . . .) 113

Pies I

In each diagram below the numbers run in pairs or in series going across or around the diagram. Insert the missing number in the blank sector.

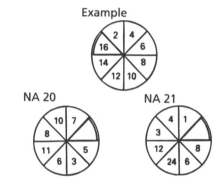

Example

NA 20   NA 21

Series II

Write in the parentheses the number that belongs at that step in the series.

NA 22   53, 47, (. . . .), 35

NA 23   33, 26, (. . . .), 12

NA 24   243, 216, (. . . .), 162

NA 25   65, 33, (. . . .), 9

NA 26   3, 4, 6, (. . . .), 18

Matrices I

In each number square below, the numbers run down and across following simple rules of arithmetic. Insert the missing number in the blank square.

Example:

1	2	3
3	4	5
5	6	7

NA 27

6	7	13
2	5	7
8	12	

NA 28

6	2	12
4	5	20
24	10	

Squares and triangles

In each set of squares the numbers are related by particular rules to produce the number in the triangle. The items in each row follow the same rule, but the rules change from row to row. Write the missing number into each blank triangle.

Example:

2 2 1 /3   5 4 1 /8   1 1 1 /1

NA 29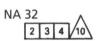

NA 30

NA 31

NA 32

NA 33

Matrices II

Insert the missing numbers in the blank squares.

NA 34

1	2	2
2	3	6
2	6	

NA 35

4	2	2
2	2	1
2	1	

Rules and shapes

Determine the rules from the first two examples in each set and then apply them in the third equation.

Example:

NA 36

NA 37

NA 38

NA 39

NA 40

NA 41

Pies II

Write the missing number into the space.

NA 42

NA 43

Double squares

The numbers in each row run in series. Write the two numbers that should appear in the blanks on the right-hand double square. In the example the left-hand numbers increase by one at each step. The right-hand numbers are multiplied by two at each step.

Example:

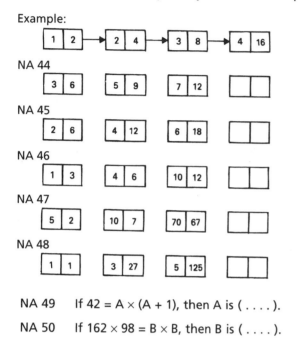

NA 49   If 42 = A × (A + 1), then A is (. . . .).

NA 50   If 162 × 98 = B × B, then B is (. . . .).

END OF NUMBER TEST A.
ANSWERS: page 26.

 PRACTICE SPATIAL TEST

Test begins here

There is no time limit, but work as quickly as you can.

PS = Practice Spatial Test

Flat turning

In each line below underline the pair of shapes which, if turned around, could represent the same shape.

Example:

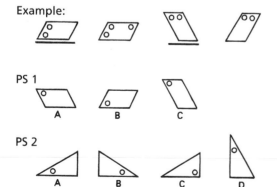

Reflected forms

In each line below, two of the shapes represent mirror images of the same shape. Underline that pair.

Example:

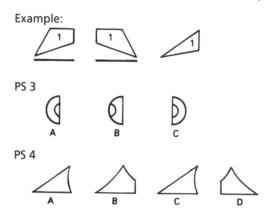

Reflecting and turning

Imagine that all the shapes in this set are transparent sheets with a heavy black line along one edge and a dot in one corner. One of the right-hand shapes represents the left-hand one, turned upside down. Write its letter in the blank circle.

Example:

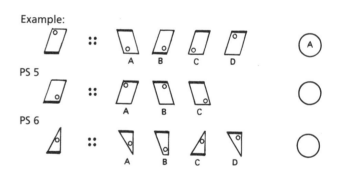

Rotation

In each row, two out of the three shapes on the left represent the same shape turned around—as on a potter's wheel, but not turned over. Underline the two shapes on the right that are rotated versions of a similar pair on the left.

Example:

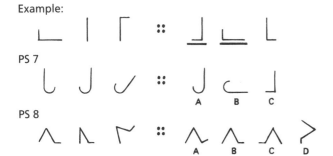

PS 7

PS 8

Fitting

The lettered shapes in the top row can be used to form the black shapes below. They may be turned over. Write one letter, or more, in the brackets to the right of each black shape to show which lettered shape or shapes can be used to form the black shape.

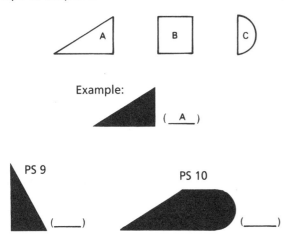

Example:

(_A_)

PS 9

(____)

PS 10

(____)

Following

The shapes on the left side form a series. Which of the lettered shapes on the right continues the series? Write the letter of the correct shape in the circle.

Example

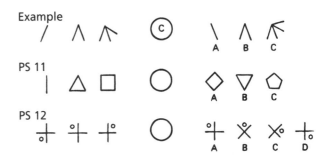

PS 11

PS 12

Counting

Each of the diagrams represents a pile of solid blocks that are all of the same size and shape. If any block is unsupported it is clearly shown as such. Some blocks are lettered. Write a number beside each letter in the column on the right to show how many blocks touch each lettered block. A whole face must touch. In the example, blocks A and B are in contact with three blocks each: now start with PS 13 and fill in the number of faces in contact with blocks A, B, and C.

Example:

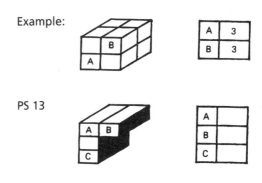

PS 13

Visualizing

Designs were drawn on some faces of these cubes. No design appears on the face of more than one cube. There are two blank faces on each cube. In each row some of the drawings are the same cube turned around. If a cube can be the same as another, assume it is the same. Write in the circle at the end of each row the least number of different cubes represented in the row. In the example, the second and third drawings are the same cube turned around.

Example:

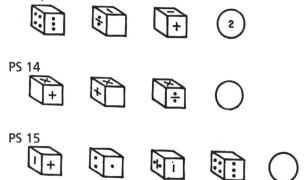

PS 14

PS 15

Analogies

In each row the first shape is related to the second shape in the same way that the third shape is related to the fourth. Underline the shape on the right that should be the fourth shape.

Example:

PS 16

PS 17

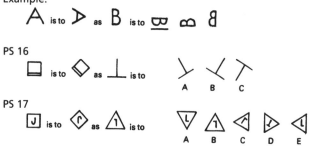

END OF PRACTICE SPATIAL TEST.

Answers to practice spatial test

PS	1	B, C
PS	2	A, D
PS	3	A, C
PS	4	B, D
PS	5	B
PS	6	A
PS	7	A, B
PS	8	B, D
PS	9	A
PS	10	A, B, C
PS	11	C (a line has two points, a triangle three, a square four, and a pentagon five)
PS	12	D (the dot moves in a clockwise direction to successive quadrants)
PS	13	A2, B1, C1
PS	14	1
PS	15	2 (the first and third drawings represent one cube and the second and fourth drawings represent another cube)
PS	16	B (the shapes are tilted to the right at an angle of 45°)
PS	17	E (the outlines of the second and fourth shapes are tilted at 45° and the inner shapes are turned upside down)

You have finished the practice test. Now make sure you have a half hour free from the risk of interruption for the timed test.

SPATIAL TEST A

Begin by writing down the exact time. You have half an hour to complete the test. When you are ready to start, read the instructions and work as quickly as you can.

SA = Spatial Test A

Flat turning

On each line below, underline the pair of shapes which, if turned around, could represent the same one.

Example:

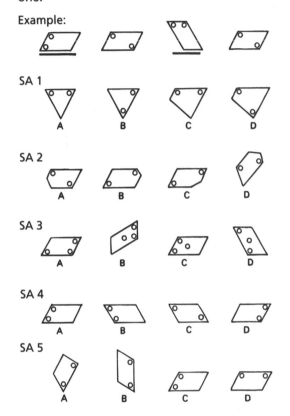

SA 1

SA 2

SA 3

SA 4

SA 5

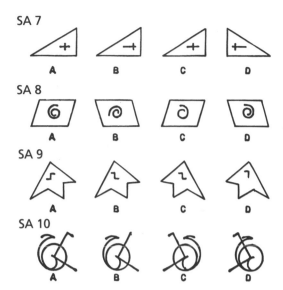

SA 7

SA 8

SA 9

SA 10

Reflecting and turning

Imagine that all the shapes in this set are transparent sheets with a heavy black line along one edge and a dot in one corner. One of the right-hand shapes represents the left-hand one, turned upside down. Write its letter in the blank circle.

Example:

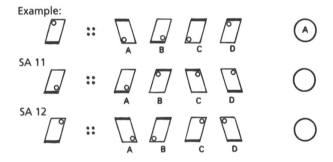

SA 11

SA 12

Reflected forms

In each of these rows, two of the shapes represent mirror images of the same shape. Underline that pair.

Example:

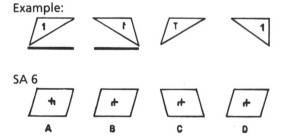

SA 6

SA 13

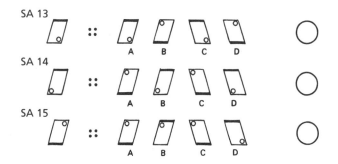

SA 14

SA 15

Potter's wheel

In each row, two of the three shapes on the left represent the same shape turned around, but not over. Underline the two shapes on the right that are rotated versions of a similar pair on the left.

Example:

SA 16

SA 17

SA 18

SA 19

SA 20

Fitting

The lettered shapes in the top row can be used to form the black shapes below. They may be turned over. Write one letter, or more, in the brackets below each black shape to show which lettered shape, or shapes, can be used to form the black shape.

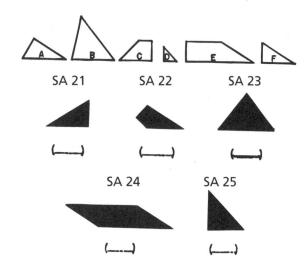

SA 21   SA 22   SA 23

(___)   (___)   (___)

SA 24   SA 25

(___)   (___)

Following

The shapes on the left form a series. Which of the lettered shapes on the right continues the series? Write the letter of the correct shape in the circle.

Example:

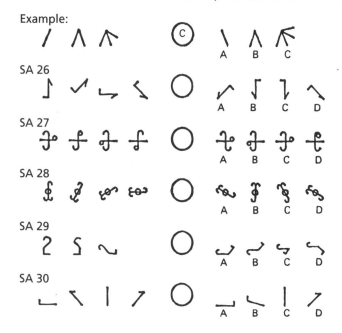

SA 26

SA 27

SA 28

SA 29

SA 30

Counting

The piles of blocks shown are solid. Any block without support is shown as such. Each diagram represents a pile of identical blocks. Write a number beside each letter in the column to show how many other blocks touch the block indicated by each letter. A whole face must touch. In SA 31 the first two letters have been matched with numbers as an example, showing that blocks A and B touch three other blocks.

Visualizing

Designs were drawn on some faces of these cubes. The same design does not appear on the face of more than one cube. There are two blank faces on each cube. In each row some of the drawings are the same cube turned around. If a cube can be the same as another, assume it is the same. Write in the circle at the end of each row the least number of different cubes represented in the row. In the example, the second and third drawings are the same cube turned around.

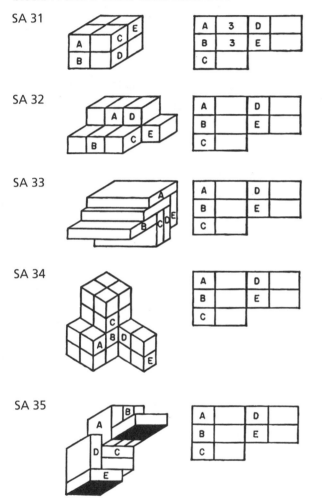

SA 31

A	3	D	
B	3	E	
C			

SA 32

A		D	
B		E	
C			

SA 33

A		D	
B		E	
C			

SA 34

A		D	
B		E	
C			

SA 35

A		D	
B		E	
C			

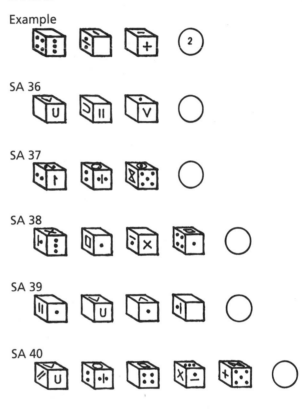

Example

SA 36

SA 37

SA 38

SA 39

SA 40

Analogies

In each row the first shape is related to the second shape in the same way that the third is related to the fourth. Underline the figure on the right that should be the fourth shape.

Example:

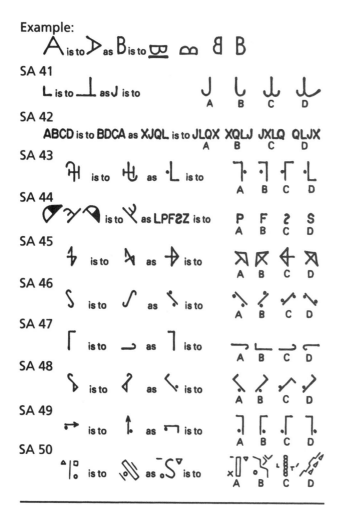

SA 41

SA 42

SA 43

SA 44

SA 45

SA 46

SA 47

SA 48

SA 49

SA 50

END OF SPATIAL TEST A.
ANSWERS: page 27.

You have now completed Cognitive Test A. Before checking your answers, you should go on to the second cognitive test, or Test B. This will take one and a half hours. Test B is designed on exactly the same lines as Test A. By taking both tests before checking, you can average the results and get a better estimate of where you stand in cognitive intelligence.

Cognitive Test B

VERBAL TEST B

Test begins here

Begin by writing down the exact time. You must complete the following 50 questions in half an hour.

VB = Verbal Test B

Analogies I

There are four terms in analogies. The first is related to the second term in the same way that the third is related to the fourth. Complete each analogy by underlining two words from the four in parentheses.

VB 1   mother is to girl as (man, father, male, boy)

VB 2   wall is to window as (glare, brick, face, eye)

VB 3   island is to water as (without, center, diagonal, perimeter)

VB 4   high is to deep as (sleep, cloud, float, coal)

VB 5   form is to content as (happiness, statue, marble, mold)

Similarities

Underline the two words in each line with the most similar meaning.

VB 6   lump, wood, ray, beam

VB 7   collect, remember, concentrate, gather

VB 8   idle, lazy, impeded, indolent

VB 9   divert, arrange, move, amuse

VB 10   antic, bucolic, drunk, rustic

Comprehension

Read the following passage. The spaces are to be filled by words from the list beneath. In each space write the letter of the word that would fill the space most sensibly. The words are to be used once only, and not all are needed.

VB 11-20 There will be (. . . .) end to the troubles (. . . .) (. . . .), or indeed, my (. . .) Glaucon, of (. . . .) itself, till philosophers become (. . .) in this (. . .) or till those we (. . .) call kings and rulers really and (. . .) (. . .) philosophers.

(A) world, (B) truly, (C) now, (D) no, (E) humanity, (F) become, (G) states, (H) an, (I) of, (J) dear, (K) kings, (L) red

Odd one out

In each group of words below, underline the two words that do not belong with the others.

VB 21   knife, razor, scissors, needle, lance

VB 22   bravery, disgust, faith, energy, fear

VB 23   prosody, geology, philosophy, physiology, physics

VB 24   glue, sieve, pickaxe, screw, string

VB 25   receptionist, draughtsman, psychiatrist, blacksmith, fitter

Links

Write in the parentheses one word that means the same in one sense as the word on the left and in another sense the same as the word on the right.

VB 26   register (**L** _ _ **T**) lean

VB 27   obligate (**T** _ _) link

VB 28   contest (**M** _ _ _ **H**) equal

VB 29   blockage (**J** _ _) preserve

VB 30   whip (**L** _ _ **H**) tie

Analogies II

Complete each analogy by writing in the parentheses one word that ends with the letters printed.

VB 31   thermometer is to temperature as clock is to (_ _ _ E)

VB 32   beyond is to without as between is to (_ _ _ _ _ N)

VB 33   egg is to ovoid as Earth is to (_ _ _ _ _ _ I D)

VB 34   potential is to actual as future is to (_ _ _ _ _ _ T)

VB 35   competition is to cooperation as rival is to (_ _ _ _ _ _ R)

Opposites

In each line below underline the two words which are most nearly opposite in meaning.

VB 36   short, length, shorten, extent, extend

VB 37   intense, extensive, majority, extreme, diffuse

VB 38   punish, vex, pinch, ignore, pacify

VB 39   reply, tell, join, disconnect, refute

VB 40   intractable, insensate, tract, obedient, disorderly

Midterms

In each line, three terms on the right should correspond to three terms on the left. Insert the missing midterm on the right.

VB 41   beginning (middle) end :: head (**W** _ _ _ _) foot

VB 42   precede (accompany) follow :: superior (**P** _ _ _) inferior

VB 43   point (cube) line :: none (**T** _ _ _ _) one

VB 44   range-finder (soldier) cannon :: probe (**S** _ _ _ _ _ _) lancet

VB 45   face (body) legs :: nose (**N** _ _ _ _) knees

Similar or opposite

In each line below, underline two words that mean most nearly either the opposite or the same as each other.

VB 46   liable, reliable, fluctuating, trustworthy, worthy

VB 47   foreign, practical, germane, useless, relevant

VB 48   relegate, reimburse, legislate, promote, proceed

VB 49   window, lucent, acrid, shining, shady

VB 50   lucubrate, bribe, indecent, spiny, obscene

END OF VERBAL TEST B.
ANSWERS: page 28.

Test begins here

NUMBER TEST B

Begin by writing down the exact time. You have half an hour to complete 50 questions.

NB = Number Test B

Equations

In each of the following equations there is one missing number that should be written in the brackets.

Example: $2 \times 12 = 6 \times (\ \overset{4}{...} \ )$

NB 1 $5 \times 9 = 15 \times (\ . \ . \ . \ . \ )$

NB 2 $16 + 7 - 29 = 5 + (\ . \ . \ . \ . \ )$

NB 3 $0.225 \times 4 = 0.75 \times (\ . \ . \ . \ . \ )$

NB 4 $0.28 \div 0.35 = 0.5 \times 0.4 \times (\ . \ . \ . \ . \ )$

NB 5 $81 + 27 = 243 \times (\ . \ . \ . \ . \ )$

Targets

In each set of missiles, there are rules that allow the target number of the missile to be formed from the numbers in the tail and wings. In the example the rule is: add the wing numbers and multiply by the tail number to get the target number. Write the answer in the blank target.

Example:

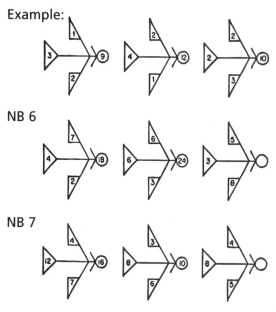

NB 6

NB 7

Series I

Each row of numbers below forms a series. Write in the parentheses at the end of each line the number which logically should follow in the series.

NB 8   2, 6, 18, 54, (. . . .)

NB 9   256, 192, 144, 108, (. . . .)

NB 10   1, 3, 7, 15, (. . . .)

NB 11   6, 13, 20, 27, (. . . .)

NB 12   49, 64, 81, 100, (. . . .)

Double rows

In each set of numbers, the same rules apply within each set to produce the numbers in the circles. Whether a number is in an upper or a lower row shows which rule applies to that number. In the example, the upper numbers in a set are added and then multiplied by the lower number to give the answer in the circle. Write the correct number in each empty circle.

Example:

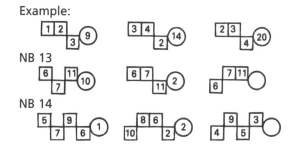

NB 13

NB 14

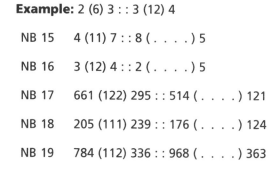

Midterms

In each line below the three numbers on the left are related in the same way as the three numbers should be on the right. Write the missing middle number on the right.

Example: 2 (6) 3 : : 3 (12) 4

NB 15   4 (11) 7 : : 8 (. . . .) 5

NB 16   3 (12) 4 : : 2 (. . . .) 5

NB 17   661 (122) 295 : : 514 (. . . .) 121

NB 18   205 (111) 239 : : 176 (. . . .) 124

NB 19   784 (112) 336 : : 968 (. . . .) 363

Pies

In each diagram below, the numbers run in pairs or series going across or around the diagram. Insert the missing number in the blank sector.

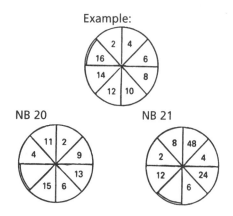

Series II

Each row of numbers forms a series. Write in the parentheses the number that logically should be there.

NB 22   52, 45, (. . . .), 31

NB 23   43, 35, (. . . .), 19

NB 24   416, 390, (. . . .), 338

NB 25   92, 79, (. . . .), 53

NB 26   1, 5, 13, (. . . .), 61

Matrices I

In each number square below, the numbers run down and across following simple rules of arithmetic. Insert the missing number in the blank square.

Example:

1	2	3
3	4	5
5	6	7

NB 27

3	4	7
7	5	12
10	9	

NB 28

2	5	10
6	3	18
12	15	

Squares and triangles

In each set of squares, the numbers are related by particular rules to produce the number in the triangle. Each row has the same set of rules, but the rules change from row to row. Write the missing number into each blank triangle.

Example:

NB 29

NB 30

NB 31

NB 32

NB 33

Matrices II

Insert the missing numbers in the blank squares.

NB 34

10,000	400	16
2,500	100	4
625	25	

NB 35

5	9	17
13	25	49
37	73	

Rules and shapes

Determine the rules from the first two examples in each set and then apply them in the third equation.

Example:

NB 36

NB 37

NB 38

NB 39

NB 40

NB 41

Pies II

Write the missing number in the space.

NB 42

NB 43

Double squares

The numbers in each row run in series. Write the two numbers that should appear in the blanks on the right-hand side double square. In the example, the left-hand numbers increase by one at each step; the right-hand numbers are multiplied by two at each step.

Example:

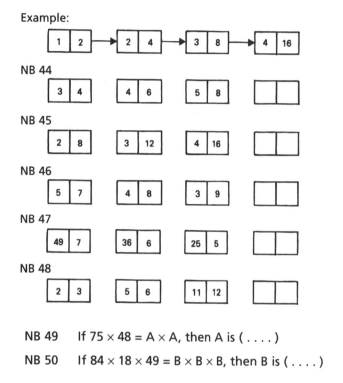

NB 44

NB 45

NB 46

NB 47

NB 48

NB 49   If $75 \times 48 = A \times A$, then A is (. . . .)

NB 50   If $84 \times 18 \times 49 = B \times B \times B$, then B is (. . . .)

END OF NUMBER TEST B.
ANSWERS: page 28.

SPATIAL TEST B

Begin by writing down the exact time. You have half an hour to complete 50 questions.

SB = Spatial Test B

Flat turning

On each line below, underline the pair of shapes which, if turned around, could represent the same one.

Example:

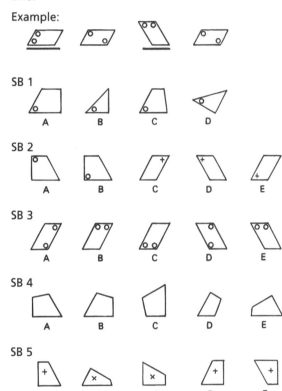

Reflected forms

On each of the following lines, two shapes represent mirror images of each other. Underline that pair.

Example:

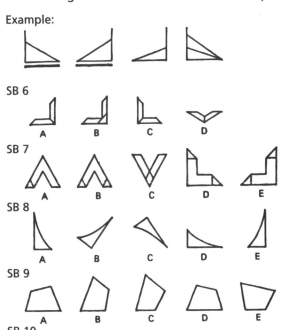

SB 6

SB 7

SB 8

SB 9

SB 10

Reflecting and turning

Imagine that all the shapes in this set are transparent sheets with a heavy black line along one edge and a dot in one corner. One of the right-hand set of shapes represents the left-hand one, turned upside-down. Write its letter in the blank circle.

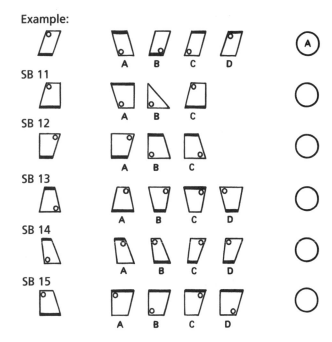

Example:

SB 11

SB 12

SB 13

SB 14

SB 15

Rotation

In each row, two of the three shapes on the left represent the same shape turned around, but not over. Underline two of the shapes on the right that are rotated versions of a similar pair on the left.

Example:

SB 16

SB 17

SB 18

SB 19

SB 20

Fitting

The lettered shapes in the top row can be used to form the black numbered shapes below. They may be turned over. Write one letter, or more, in the brackets below each black shape to show which lettered shape, or shapes, can be used to make the black shape.

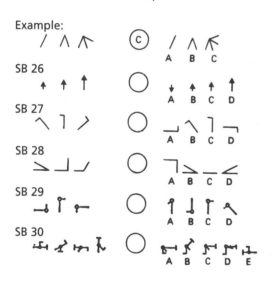

Following

The shapes on the left form a series. Which of the shapes on the right continues the series? Write the letter of the correct shape in the circle.

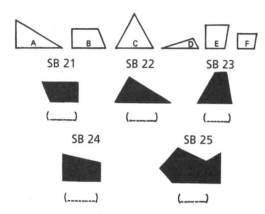

Counting

The piles of blocks shown are solid. Any block without support is shown as such. Each diagram below represents a pile of blocks, all of the same size and shape. Some blocks are lettered. Write a number beside each letter in the column on the right to show how many blocks touch each lettered block. A whole face must touch. The first letter has been matched with a number as an example to show that block A touches three other blocks.

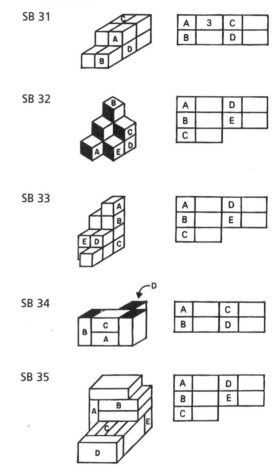

Visualizing

Designs were drawn on some faces of these cubes. No design appears on the face of more than one cube. There are two blank faces on each cube. In each row some of the drawings are the same cube turned around. If a cube can be the same as another, assume it is the same. Write in the circle at the end of each row the least number of different cubes represented in the row. In the example, the second and third drawings are the same cube turned around.

Example:

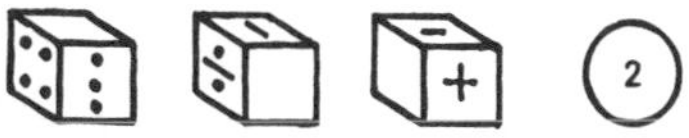
2

SB 36

SB 37

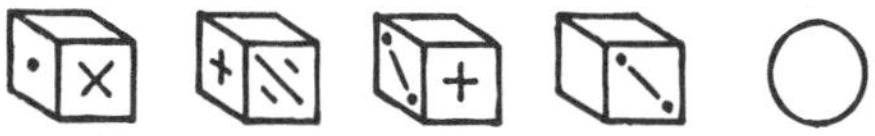

SB 38

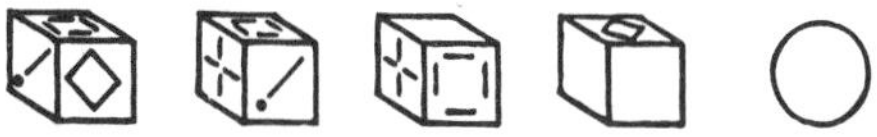

SB 39

SB 40

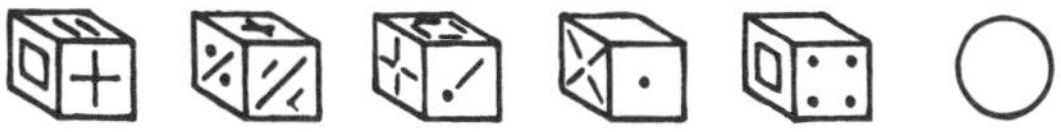

Analogies

In each row, the first shape is related to the second shape in the same way that the third is related to the fourth. Underline the figure on the right that should be the fourth shape.

Example:

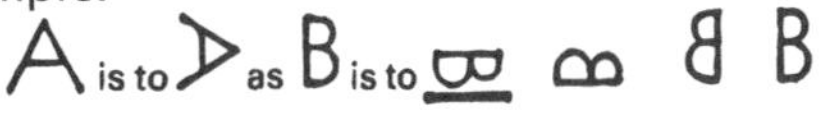
A is to
as B is to

SB 41

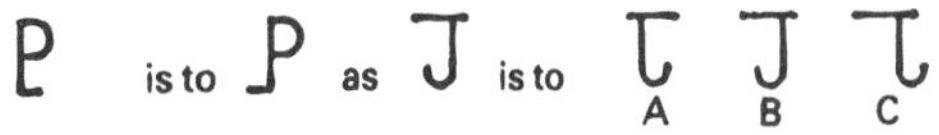
is to
as
is to
A B C

SB 42

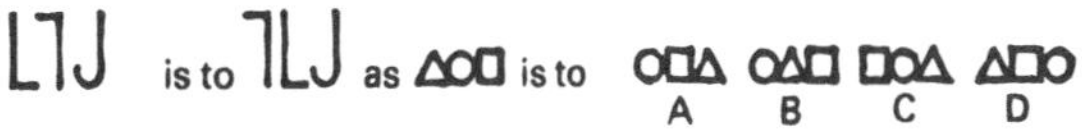
is to
as
is to
A B C D

SB 43

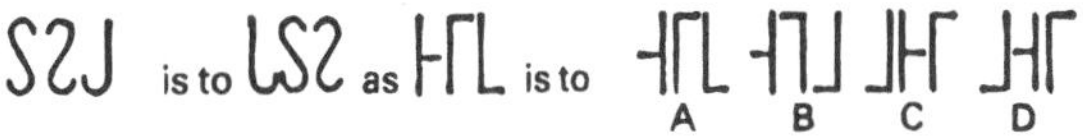
is to
as
is to
A B C D

SB 44

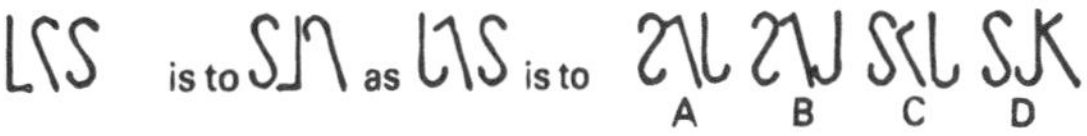
is to
as
is to
A B C D

SB 45

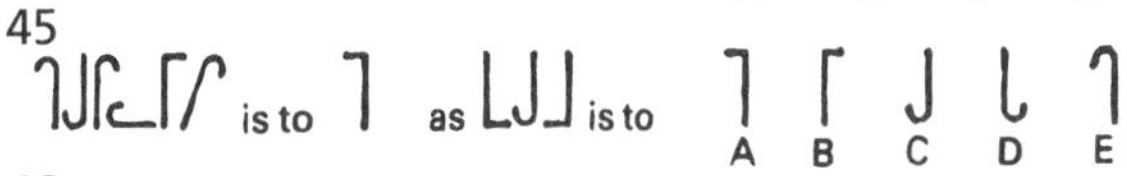
is to
as
is to
A B C D E

SB 46

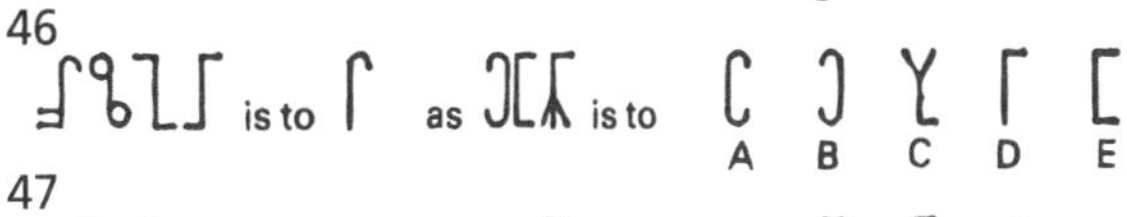
is to
as
is to
A B C D E

SB 47

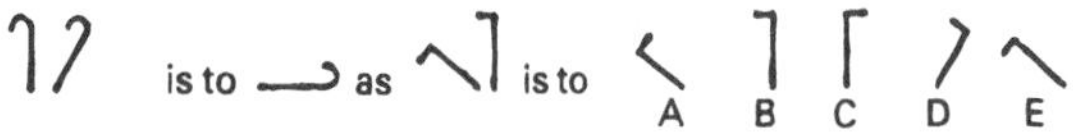
is to
as
is to
A B C D E

SB 48

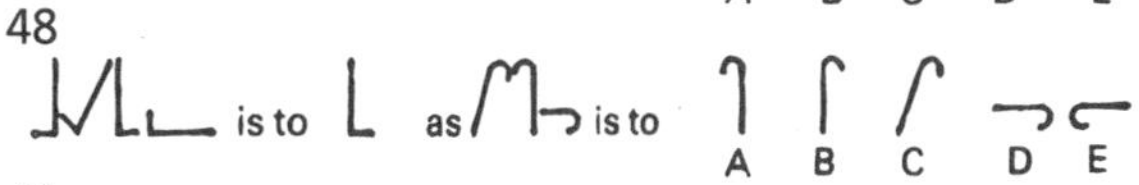
is to
as
is to
A B C D E

SB 49

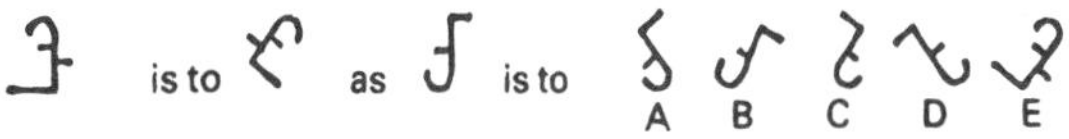
is to
as
is to
A B C D E

SB 50

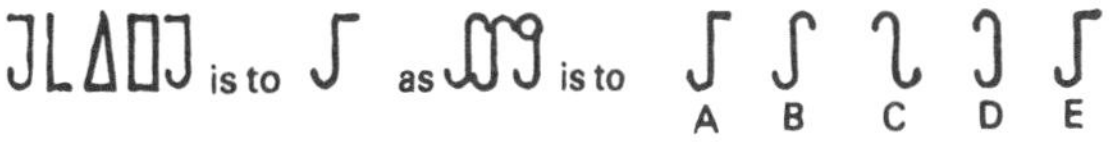
is to
as
is to
A B C D E

END OF SPATIAL TEST B.

ANSWERS: page 29.

Answers and Evaluation (Tests A and B)

COGNITIVE TEST A

✓ Answers to verbal test A

Answers begins here

VA 1   teacup, saucer
VA 2   leader, follower (in the action of sewing, the thread follows the needle)
VA 3   rejoice, mourn (opposites)
VA 4   window, view (a floor provides support and a window provides a view)
VA 5   eyes, window (veils cover eyes as curtains cover windows)
VA 6   divulge, reveal
VA 7   blessing, benediction
VA 8   intelligence, tidings ("intelligence" in the sense of "news")
VA 9   tale, story
VA 10   punish, chastise
VA 11   F (equally)
VA 12   C (diminution)
VA 13   L (write)
VA 14   D (public)
VA 15   E (remembrance)
VA 16   H (unless)
VA 17   G (new)
VA 18   I (forgetful)
VA 19   K (merit)
VA 20   B (fame)
VA 21   sea lion, whale (both mammals, the others are fish)
VA 22   cloth, tinfoil (the others are made of compressed fibers)
VA 23   arrow, bullet (the others are used in the hand)
VA 24   quick, full (the others mean "more so")
VA 25   fear, love (the others are detected by the senses)
VA 26   dart
VA 27   form
VA 28   press
VA 29   fine
VA 30   fire
VA 31   deny, affirm
VA 32   veil, expose
VA 33   frank, secretive
VA 34   aggravate, improve
VA 35   primeval, ultimate

VA 36   is
VA 37   sometimes
VA 38   few
VA 39   transient
VA 40   ripe
VA 41   mercurial, phlegmatic (opposites)
VA 42   object, demur (synonyms)
VA 43   tenacious, irresolute (opposites)
VA 44   literally, veritably (synonyms)
VA 45   heap, hole (opposites)
VA 46   selfish
VA 47   intrepid
VA 48   discord
VA 49   aloof
VA 50   yolk

Answers to number test A

NA 1   4
NA 2   −17
NA 3   .05
NA 4   .2
NA 5 $^1/_{128}$ (0.0078125)
NA 6   2 (divide the tail number by the sum of the numbers in the wings)
NA 7   11 (multiply the wing numbers and add the tail number)
NA 8   48 (double the previous number)
NA 9   16 (each number is $^2/_3$ the previous number)
NA 10   33 (add to each successive number an amount double the difference between the previous pair of numbers)
NA 11   31 (add sixes)
NA 12   49 (the numbers are, successively, squares of 3, 4, 5, 6, and 7)
NA 13   9 (add upper squares; subtract lower squares)
NA 14   2 (multiply numbers in upper squares; subtract lower squares)
NA 15   11 (add numbers outside brackets to give numbers inside)
NA 16   9 (multiply outer numbers to obtain inner number)
NA 17   16 (inner number is sum of square roots of outer numbers)
NA 18   168 (inner number is the largest common factor of outer numbers)

NA 19   656 (inner number is twice the sum of outer numbers)

NA 20   2 (opposite numbers make 13)

NA 21   2 (the product of opposite numbers is 24)

NA 22   41 (each number is 6 less than the preceding one)

NA 23   19 (each number is 7 less than the preceding one)

NA 24   189 (each number is 27 less than the preceding one)

NA 25   17 (each number is half the preceding number after one is added to the preceding number)

NA 26   10 (each number is twice the preceding one, minus two)

NA 27   20 (first column plus second gives third, first row plus second gives third)

NA 28   240 (in rows and columns, the first number and second are multiplied to give the third)

NA 29   5 (first two numbers minus the third gives the fourth)

NA 30   1 (multiply the first two numbers and subtract the third to obtain the fourth)

NA 31   3 (add the second and third numbers and subtract the first to give the fourth)

NA 32   5 (multiply the first two and add the third)

NA 33   3 (multiply the first two numbers and divide by the third)

NA 34   12 (in rows and columns, the first number multiplied by the second gives the third)

NA 35   2 (in rows and columns, the first number divided by the second gives the third)

NA 36   5 (the sum of numbers in triangles gives the answer)

NA 37   2 (the difference of numbers in triangles)

NA 38   12 (the product of numbers in triangle and square)

NA 39   1 (the number in the triangle is divided by the number in the circle)

NA 40   4 (add numbers in triangles and subtract number in inverted triangle)

NA 41   6 (multiply numbers in the triangle and the square, and divide by the number in the circle)

NA 42   4 (opposite numbers add up to 18)

NA 43   36 (opposite numbers multiplied give 36)

NA 44   9, 15 (the first number in each domino is two more and the second number is three more than in the domino before)

NA 45   8, 24 (the first number in the domino is two more and the second six more than in the domino before)

NA 46   22, 24 (the second number in each domino is twice that in the domino before, and the first number is 2 less than the second)

NA 47   4690, 4687 (the first number in each domino is the product of the numbers in the domino before; the second is three less)

NA 48   7, 343 (the first numbers in the domino are the natural series of odd numbers and the second are their cubes)

NA 49   6

NA 50   126

Answers to spatial test A

SA 1   A, B

SA 2   A, D

SA 3   B, C

SA 4   A, D

SA 5   B, D

SA 6   A, C

SA 7   B, D

SA 8   A, D

SA 9   A, C

SA 10   A, C

SA 11   C

SA 12   A

SA 13   D

SA 14   C

SA 15   D

SA 16   A, D

SA 17   B, D

SA 18   B, D

SA 19   A, C

SA 20   B, D

SA 21   A

SA 22   D, F

SA 23   B

SA 24   E, F

SA 25   C, D

SA 26   B

SA 27   C

SA 28   D

SA 29   D

SA 30   A (the lines resemble clock hands)

SA 31   C3, D3, E3

SA 32   A3, B3, C2, D2, E1

SA 33   A2, B2, C3, D3, E3

SA 34   A3, B5, C4, D3, E2

SA 35   A4, B4, C5, D4, E2

SA 36   one

SA 37   two (the first two represent the same cube)

SA 38   two (the first and third, and the second and fourth, have the same design on one face and so must be the same cube in each case)

SA 39	two (the first three represent the same cube)
SA 40	three (the different designs could be the opposite three faces of two pairs and a single, therefore we assume that they are)
SA 41	D
SA 42	A
SA 43	B (the feature face of the shape is turned from left to right and then put at the opposite end)
SA 44	C (the second shape is the same as the odd one from the first set of shapes)
SA 45	D
SA 46	C
SA 47	A
SA 48	D
SA 49	B
SA 50	B (long form tilted, loose features move to center)

COGNITIVE TEST B

Answers to verbal test B

VB 1	father, boy
VB 2	face, eye
VB 3	center, perimeter
VB 4	cloud, coal (one is found high above earth, the other deep within it)
VB 5	statue, marble (these are examples of form and content)
VB 6	ray, beam
VB 7	collect, gather
VB 8	lazy, indolent
VB 9	divert, amuse
VB 10	bucolic, rustic
VB 11	D (no)
VB 12	I (of)
VB 13	G (states)
VB 14	J (dear)
VB 15	E (humanity)
VB 16	K (kings)
VB 17	A (world)
VB 18	C (now)
VB 19	B (truly)
VB 20	F (become)
VB 21	needle, lance (the others have sharp edges)
VB 22	disgust, fear (emotions; the others are virtues)
VB 23	prosody, philosophy (aspects of literary culture; the others are sciences)
VB 24	sieve, pickaxe (these separate things; the others fix them together)
VB 25	receptionist, psychiatrist (main work is dealing with people; the others deal with things)

VB 26	list
VB 27	tie
VB 28	match
VB 29	jam
VB 30	lash
VB 31	time
VB 32	within
VB 33	spheroid (ovoid means egg-shaped; a spheroid is the shape of the earth)
VB 34	present
VB 35	partner
VB 36	shorten, extend
VB 37	intense, diffuse
VB 38	vex, pacify
VB 39	join, disconnect
VB 40	intractable, obedient
VB 41	waist
VB 42	peer
VB 43	three (points have no dimensions, cubes three, and lines one)
VB 44	surgeon (probes and lancets are tools of surgeons as weapons are of soldiers)
VB 45	navel (approximate center of body)
VB 46	reliable, trustworthy (synonyms)
VB 47	germane, relevant (synonyms)
VB 48	relegate, promote (opposites)
VB 49	lucent, shining (synonyms)
VB 50	indecent, obscene (synonyms)

Answers to number test B

NB 1	3
NB 2	−11
NB 3	1.2
NB 4	4
NB 5	$^4/_9$ (0.4 recurring)
NB 6	43 (multiply wing numbers and add tail number)
NB 7	12 (multiply wing numbers and subtract tail number)
NB 8	162 (each number is three times the preceding number)
NB 9	81 (each number is three-quarters the preceding number)
NB 10	31 (each number is twice that before, plus one)
NB 11	34 (each number is seven more than the number before)
NB 12	121 (the series is: 7×7, 8×8, 9×9, 10×10, and 11×11)
NB 13	12 (add upper numbers and subtract lower numbers)
NB 14	3 (add upper numbers and subtract lower numbers)

NB 15 13 (the inner number is the sum of the outer numbers)

NB 16 10 (the inner number is the product of the outer numbers)

NB 17 131 (the inner number is one-third of the difference between the outer numbers)

NB 18 75 (the inner number is a quarter of the sum of the others)

NB 19 121 (the inner number is the largest number that is a factor of the outer numbers)

NB 20 8 (opposite numbers add up to 17)

NB 21 1 (the product of opposite numbers is 48)

NB 22 38 (each number is 7 less than the preceding number)

NB 23 27 (each number is 8 less than the preceding number)

NB 24 364 (each number is 26 less than the preceding number)

NB 25 66 (each number is 13 less than the preceding number)

NB 26 29 (each number is twice the number before, plus three)

NB 27 19 (in columns and rows, the third number is the sum of the first two)

NB 28 180 (in columns and rows, the third number is the product of the first two)

NB 29 1 (add the first two numbers and subtract the third)

NB 30 11 (multiply the first two numbers and subtract the third)

NB 31 1 (add the first and third numbers and subtract the second)

NB 32 12 (multiply the first two numbers and add the third)

NB 33 16 (multiply the first two numbers and divide by the third)

NB 34 1 (divide by 2 going down and divide by 5 going across after taking the square roots)

NB 35 145 (after subtracting 1 from all numbers, multiply by 3 going down and multiply by 2 going across)

NB 36 7 (add numbers inside the triangles)

NB 37 2 (the middle number is the difference between numbers in the triangles)

NB 38 18 (the middle number is the product of the others)

NB 39 7 (divide the first number by the third)

NB 40 3 (subtract the fourth number from the sum of the first and third)

NB 41 30 (the second number is the product of the others)

NB 42 13 (the sum of opposite numbers is 22)

NB 43 1 (the product of opposite numbers is 40)

NB 44 6, 10 (the first number in each domino is one more, and the second two more, than in the domino before)

NB 45 5, 20 (the first number in each domino is one more than in the domino before; the second number is four times the first)

NB 46 2, 10 (the first number in each domino is one less, and the second one more, than in the domino before)

NB 47 16, 4 (the second number in each domino is one less than in the domino before; the first number is the square of the second)

NB 48 23, 24 (the second number in each domino is twice the number in the domino before; the first number is one less than the second)

NB 49 60

NB 50 42

Answers to spatial test B

SB 1 B, D

SB 2 C, E

SB 3 B, C

SB 4 A, C

SB 5 A, E

SB 6 A, C

SB 7 D, E

SB 8 A, E

SB 9 A, D

SB 10 A, D

SB 11 A

SB 12 C

SB 13 B

SB 14 D

SB 15 B

SB 16 A, D

SB 17 A, B

SB 18 B, D

SB 19 B, C

SB 20 A, C

SB 21 B

SB 22 A

SB 23 D, C

SB 24 E, F

SB 25 A, B, D

SB 26 D

SB 27 A

SB 28 C

SB 29 B

SB 30 C

SB 31   B2, C3, D4

SB 32   A1, B1, C2, D3, E2

SB 33   A1, B3, C3, D3, E3

SB 34   A4, B2, C4, D2

SB 35   A5, B3, C5, D4, E6

SB 36   two (the first two represent the same cube)

SB 37   two (the first represents a cube different from the rest)

SB 38   one

SB 39   three (the first two represent the same cube)

SB 40   four (the first and second represent the same cube)

SB 41   C (the foot of the shape is turned from one side to the other)

SB 42   B (the first and second units in the shape change places)

SB 43   C (the last unit becomes the first and is transformed into its mirror image)

SB 44   D (the first unit becomes second and is transformed into its mirror image; the last unit becomes first; and the second unit becomes last and its head is turned around)

SB 45   D (the shape most unlike the rest is transformed into its mirror image)

SB 46   D (pick out the head of the shape whose head differs from its foot)

SB 47   D (the series proceeds by units successively turning in a clockwise direction)

SB 48   A (pick out the shape least resembling the others in terms of clockwise rotation)

SB 49   C (the first shape is transformed into the second shape by turning it in a clockwise direction 45° after it has been transformed into a mirror image)

SB 50   D (pick a shape that has a twin and turn its head from one side to the other)

COGNITIVE TEST RESULTS

To determine your IQ (or percentile) from your score, whether you did one or both tests:

(1)   Add up the number of questions you got completely right on the Verbal Test(s) and enter it on the "Test total form." If you did both tests, enter both scores.

(2)   Now do the same for the Spatial Test(s).

(3)   Now do the same for the Number Test(s).

(4)   Multiply the verbal score by three and then add it to the other scores to make up your final raw score (either for one test or for both).

(5)   Now refer to the Results Table.

The Results Table allows you to determine your IQ or percentile rating, by finding your raw score and looking across the table.

There are two columns for the raw score against IQ and percentile, one for those who took both tests and one for those who took only one of them.

Read from the appropriate column across to the IQ and percentile score.

Find the nearest score to your own score and read across to the correct column (1 test or 2 tests). Read out IQ and percentile.

The percentile rating tells you what proportion of the test sample population would have scored as well as you did or lower. For example, if you are on the 90th percentile, then 90% scored the same or less than you. Only 10% scored higher. If you are on the 50th percentile (IQ 100), then you have exactly the average score.

The Intelligence Quotient or IQ is a confusing technical expression that should never have become popular. Strictly, it applies to children and only by extrapolation to adults. It is the mental age multiplied by 100 divided by the actual age. If a child of 10 can perform as well as the average child of 15, his or her IQ is

$$\frac{15 \times 100}{10} = 150$$

The average IQ is (naturally, therefore) 100.

Unfortunately, different psychologists produce different results from Binet's primitive scheme, so that an IQ score means different things on different tests according to the standard deviation.

A preferable way of judging IQ is by percentile rating. Your percentile rating is that percentage of the general population (upon whom the test was standardized) which your performance equals or excels.

Test total form

Raw score

Number Test	A	☐
	B	☐
Spatial Test	A	☐
	B	☐

Verbal test   A   ☐
B   ☐

Verbal total   ☐   × 3   =   ☐

Total raw score   ☐

IQ = ☐   Percentile = ☐

Raw score

One test	Both tests	IQ	Per-centile
5	11	81	10th
9	19	82	12th
13	27	83	13th
17	35	84	14th
21	43	85	16th
25	50	86	18th
29	58	87	20th
33	66	88	21st
37	74	89	23rd
41	82	90	25th
45	90	91	27th
48	97	92	30th
52	105	93	32rd
56	113	94	34th
60	121	95	37th
64	129	96	40th
68	137	97	42nd
72	144	98	45th
76	152	99	47th
80	160	100	50th
84	168	101	52nd
88	176	102	55th
92	184	103	58th
95	191	104	60th
99	199	105	63rd
103	207	106	66th
107	215	107	68th
111	223	108	70th
115	231	109	73rd
119	238	110	76th
123	246	111	77th
127	254	112	79th

Raw score

One test	Both tests	IQ	Per-centile	
131	262	113	81st	
135	270	114	82nd	
139	278	115	84th	
142	285	116	86th	
146	293	117	87th	
150	301	118	88th	
154	309	119	90th	
158	317	120	91st	
162	325	121	92nd	
166	332	122	93rd	
170	340	123	94th	
174	348	124	94th	← _Worth a try for Mensa_
178	356	125	95th	
182	364	126	96th	
186	372	127	96th	
189	379	128	97th	
193	387	129	97th	
197	395	130	98th	
201	403	131	98th	
205	411	132		
209	419	133		
213	426	134		_Mensa level_
217	434	135		
221	442	136		
225	450	137		
229	458	138	99th	
233	466	139		
236	473	140		
240	481	141		
244	489	142		
248	497	143		
250	500	144		